I'm Too Polite, Grandma

Sandra Schofield

Published by New Generation Publishing in 2022

First Edition

ISBN 978-1-80031-053-7

www.newgeneration-publishing.com

New Generation Publishing

This book is dedicated to the memory of my mother

Joyce Schofield née Mitchell

13/6/1928 – 2/9/1965

Chapter One: A Chance Encounter

My grandparents Ethel and John Mitchell married in 1928. At the time my grandma was expecting my mother, Joyce. This fact was kept as a family secret and I only found out about it when I grew up and started to research my family tree.

So then I realised that Grandma had been very secretive with me about her life, as later on other family facts were revealed.

My story begins with the marriage of my parents Geoffrey and Joyce Schofield (nee Mitchell) who were married in 1953 at St Mary's Church on St Mary's Way in Rochdale.

My parents first knew each other when they attended St Peter's Primary School in Rochdale.

This was in 1933 when they were both five years old.

My mother left here to attend Brown Hill School on Heights Lane in Rochdale. She left St Peter's School due to ill health. According to school records which I have read, my mother Joyce left St Peter's Primary School to attend an open air school because of her bronchitis and continuing chest problems. She was eleven years old at the time.

Years later they met up again at a dance. It was at the Carlton ballroom in Rochdale. The year was 1951.

Geoffrey was on leave from the Canadian army when they met up and Joyce was a winder at John Bright's mill on Whitworth Road in Rochdale.

As well as having bronchitis, she worked in a cotton mill which was full of cotton bits floating in the air, so I am surprised that she worked here as she had already attended open air school because of her chest problems.

When I asked Grandma about this she said that there were very few career opportunities for women around this time.

I rather thought it showed some naivety on the part of my grandma to send my mother to work there.

She was a beautiful young woman who was looking for a husband around this time.

My father Geoffrey said to me that Joyce had come up to him at the dance and said, "It's Geoffrey Schofield from St Peter's Primary School!"

Geoffrey said that he remembered her from primary school even though they had both grown up.

My father was pleased that someone from his school had recognised him.

"Hiya Joyce, it's been a long time since we last saw each other! How are you getting on?"

So the happy couple began by re-introducing themselves and they ended up waltzing on the dance floor together for most of the evening. This was how people used to court each other in 1953.

The Carlton was on Great George Street in Rochdale and this building later became Liquid Rock. In those days, everyone was taught how to do the waltz. Geoffrey was good at the moves and used to show us them years later!

Many a Rochdale couple must have met in this romantic building during the 1950s.

Geoffrey told Joyce that he was on leave from the army and that he was stationed in Canada. My mother must have thought that it was romantic that he was on leave from the army and how dashingly handsome he was as well!

Both Geoffrey and Joyce were at the dance without a friend which I thought was remarkable when Geoffrey told me this.

Grandma also told me that Joyce would often go to dances alone. She did not have a sister and her brother was five years younger than her so he had his own circle of friends.

Joyce had had friends to go out with but they had all married young and in those days couples were married by their teens and early twenties. Joyce, at the grand old age of twenty-five was beginning to feel that she was going to be left on the shelf, so to speak. Geoffrey was still available because he had been away in the army.

So they began their courtship and fell in love.

When they were first married they lived at 55 Watkin Street in Rochdale.

They had bought their first home for just two thousand pounds! This was the amount that their mortgage was, minus the deposit.

Joyce carried on working in the cotton mill, excitedly saving towards a deposit on a home to live in with Geoffrey.

Geoffrey was writing love letters to Joyce all the way from Canada, saying he was looking forward to their future together.

Their wedding was in 1953 and Grandma said they were the only couple in the family that were not pregnant when it was their wedding day!

Geoffrey wanted to come out of the army. He had been doing his national service, which had been brought in after the Second World War.

National service involved young men training for the army to develop skills during the Cold War for

defence of the country in case any more wars broke out. Thankfully there have been no more world wars.

Before moving to this address Geoffrey had lived with his father Major Schofield at 50 Windmill Street in Rochdale. Joyce had lived with her mother Ethel and her father John at 4 Leamington Street, Rochdale.

So off went the happy couple Joyce and Geoffrey to their new home.

Both Joyce and Geoffrey had family members in this area of Rochdale and this is how the couple had met through first meeting as small primary school children in the same class, then they lost contact at school but still lived in the same area of Rochdale.

Both my mother and father were above average looking. My father was a small man with blonde hair and a very good bone structure, with high cheekbones and an oval-shaped face.

My beautiful mother Joyce boasted curly locks of streaming black hair and blue eyes. Grandma used to say that the whites of her eyes were a pale shade of blue because she was so beautiful. She was a beautiful person inside as well as on the outside. My mother had been selfless, Grandma said.

Geoffrey could not wait to come out of the army and begin a civilian life with my mum. This I was told later on by my grandma.

My mother had kept her white lace wedding dress in the wardrobe for years after she got married. I remember seeing it in her wardrobe when my sister Anne and I were looking for stiletto heeled shoes to dress up in!

During their courtship Joyce had been saving up her wages to pay for a deposit on a house and they put a deposit on 55 Watkin Street Rochdale.

This was a two-bedroomed terraced house with no bathroom and a back yard. Downstairs, it comprised a small kitchen and living room.

Grandma said that Geoffrey looked forward to coming home from Canada to live with Joyce, that he said to her in his love letters home that he marked days off the calendar as each day ended and his time in the army came to an end and he came home to marry his love, my mother.

Chapter Two: Early Childhood Memories

Five years later their first daughter Anne was born, in May 1956.

They were very happy but Geoffrey had hoped for a boy. Nevertheless, they both loved their daughter, who they had named after Princess Anne.

They went on holiday to Torquay after Anne was born. Some other family members went as well.

These were Joyce's parents Ethel and John Mitchell, John's sister Olive Wild and her husband James Wild and their two sons Dennis and David, who were nearly grown up, and Joyce's younger brother Jack, who was younger than Joyce by five years.

Geoffrey had trained as a clerk in the army and he managed to get a job at Rochdale railway station in the station office. He worked as a wages clerk.

This was back in the days when trains were used to deliver goods to towns. These were mostly steam trains at the time.

Our father Geoffrey liked the outdoors and as a boy he had walked everywhere wherever possible and hardly ever caught a bus. As a result of this he was very fit and active.

Every weekend as children we would be taken on outings with our father. For as long as I can remember we went on outings at weekends either with just our father or with both our parents. I think Geoffrey encouraged Joyce to get out of the house as well. We would go to Falinge Park where we could play on the swings. We went on picnics to Blackstone Edge where there was a white house. It was a public house but we never went in it because children were not allowed inside. We had a picnic nearby and played in the countryside but I was always fascinated by the big white house. I would imagine who lived inside it.

Our father took us on outings on Saturdays. This was usually to the library where we would run around screaming before picking a book to borrow for a week until we came again. Because we were interested in reading we all became good readers. We were encouraged by our parents to read books. Anne and I loved fairy stories like Cinderella, Snow White and the Sleeping Beauty; these stories were written by Walt Disney and provided a perfect scenario for girls to view the adult world of finding a husband and all of the romance that goes with it.

One of these outings was to go and visit our grandfather, Major Schofield, who lived at 50 Windmill Street in Rochdale.

As with many of our outings we walked all the way there and back. We walked from where we lived on Howard Street into the town centre of Rochdale then up Drake Street and past high level then turned into Woodbine Street along Crawford Street and onto Windmill Street. We would go past a play area with some swings but we were not allowed to go on the swings and we had to keep walking!

Major Schofield had married Ada Blackburn, my paternal grandmother, who I never met. He was a proud man who wore a flat cap and a long raincoat when he went out. He had worked all his life in the mill before retiring. It's strange to think that all the time I knew him he was retired.

Major Schofield was born in 1901 and died in 1981 aged seventy-nine years.

After three years of marriage the couple had split up and Major was left to bring up my father Geoffrey as a single parent. He was helped to bring Geoffrey by his sister Mary

Dixon. She was married to Benjamin Dixon but she had no children of her own.

They split up in 1931 so this would have been before the welfare state was introduced in 1948.

Therefore, I believe that my paternal grandmother left my father when he was three years old because she would not have been able to look after him in a financial way.

Apparently she left because she met another man. My father never got over this fact and he refused to take us to see her but I always wanted to see her and know more about her. My father was angry that his mother had walked out on him and his father. That was that and I was never allowed to question it.

I wish, however, that I did get to know more about her because she was my grandmother and therefore she was a part of me. My father Geoffrey must have had a memory of her but I had no

memory of her at all though I knew that she must have existed. I often wandered if David had got his nose from her. David had the cutest button nose that resembled Winston Churchill's.

I remember my grandad Schofield as a character who made me laugh a lot. I think he was rather a comedian without meaning to be.

He had an open coal fire and sometimes when we visited him he would make toast for us. He cut the bread from a loaf of bread and toasted it with a long fork over the fire until it went brown. This was normal for him. He had never owned a cooker or a freezer.

He must have been a good soul to have brought my dad up all by himself. His house was very homely. He would pass the toast round and we would share it, as well as the cocoa!

One Sunday in 1962 we arrived to visit him and found him at the kitchen sink rubbing fairy soap on his shirt collar and cuffs before he handwashed his shirt. The bar of fairy soap was green and rectangular like the shape of a small brick.

He hung his shirt out in the back yard on the washing line with two wooden dolly pegs.

Also in his back yard was the outside toilet. Our grandad made his own loo roll by recycling his newspaper. He cut the paper into squares with scissors and hung up his homemade loo roll using string. This was another thing that we found hilarious.

Whenever we had a chippy tea it came wrapped in an old newspaper!

We only ever had a chippy tea when we visited Grandad Major Schofield.

He showed us a card game called Clock Face where the cards are placed in a circle just like a clock face with the numbers.

At the end of the game there is a clock face with the cards.

Grandad Schofield also showed us a game of cards called Patience. He said he had shown it to Geoffrey our father when he was a boy but that Geoffrey had hated the game!

First, shuffle the cards.

The cards are placed into twelve lines. One card is placed in the first line. Two cards are placed in the second line, three in the third line and four in the fourth and so on until the twelfth line has twelve cards placed in it. Next thing to do is turn over the card that is in the first line. Secondly, turn over the first card that is in the second line, then turn over the first card that is in the third line and place it in position 1-12.

Every fifteen minutes a grandfather clock would strike out the time and every hour the clock would strike out the hour.

It was a low chime that felt reassuring.

Eczema is a hereditary skin complaint that runs in families. It can be weepy or dry, and in our case it is dry. It affects every second generation. But there may only be one sufferer at one time.

My grandad Schofield had very dry skin eczema that would sometimes itch. He was prescribed Synalar cream from his doctor. This is a mild hydrocortisone to stop itching and help with inflammation

Grandad Schofield never married again after his wife Ada left him when my father Geoffrey was three in 1931.

By this time my father was just three years old. He said he saw his mother from time to time whilst he was growing up and felt sad that his parents were no longer together.

His mother Ada had remarried shortly after she had left his father. It is believed that she had some more children. Geoffrey said that he lost contact with his mother. He found it difficult to talk about her and her new family.

Her maiden name was Blackburn, so she was named Ada Blackburn and I never met her even though she was my paternal grandmother. She married Major in 1927 and they split up in 1931.

Ada's second husband was called Butler (my father Geoffrey told me this).

Another outing was to take us shopping for groceries at Redman's in Yorkshire Street in Rochdale.

On the way there we crossed through Baillie Street in Rochdale town centre. There was a model shop with a train on a track in the window of the shop. Our father inserted an old penny in the slot and the train set off around the track and chuffed up and down and round the track. It was great entertainment and our father loved it as well! It went on for several minutes.

At the other end of Baillie Street were some old toilets. They were down some steps and were decorated with white tiles everywhere and a strong smell of disinfectant. The toilets had enormous wooden doors with gaps under the doors. To open the door, you had to place an old penny in the slot on the door. The toilets had an attendant whose job it was to clean them.

Chapter Three: Cronkeyshaw Primary School

During the week all three of us attended Cronkeyshaw Primary School but David was only there for a year before the catastrophe happened.

I had been there for three years and I excelled at reading. My favourites were Janet and John books which taught children to read in ITA. I was reading a full book a day. Miss Smith, the teacher, said to me, "Take the book home and read it to your parents and then bring the book here again tomorrow."

Miss Smith said she only expected me to be reading a page a day but I read the full book and I really enjoyed reading and writing from a very young age.

I ran home with the book and read it to my mum, page by page, then the next day I took the book to Miss Smith and read it back to her. Then I would get another reading book. I was ahead of the class with reading.

I learned to write in ITA and I was writing by the time that I was five years old.

Also on Saturdays we were taken to the children's library on the esplanade in Rochdale town centre and both our parents took us all there on Saturdays.

It is a fantastic building with statues on the brickwork. It is now called Touchstones.

Sometimes we would get fed up and run around screaming. If Anne ran around screaming, I was sure to copy her and run around screaming too and then David would join in too so at times we must have been quite hard work for our parents. Despite our form of play we all learned to read when we were five years old.

After a few months, Joyce and Geoffrey decided to try for another baby and when Anne was only nine months old, Joyce became pregnant again at the end of February 1957.

They wanted a boy so that they would have a boy and a girl.

When the baby arrived, I was a girl and not the boy that had been wanted by my parents.

I weighed 8 lbs which is big for a girl, especially in those days.

I was named Sandra by my mother. She named me after her best friend, who was a Scottish lady.

My sister Anne said she remembered me being born and she was told to play in the back yard of the house.

I am sure she is mistaken about this because most people don't have recollection of a memory until they are three years old and when I was born Anne would only have been eighteen months old.

This memory that she had of being sent out to play in the back yard must have come from our brother David's birth. He was born in 1959 when Anne was three and a half years old. I was two years old at the time.

As people do not have a recall of memory until they are three years of age, I am sure that it must have been David's birth that she remembered.

Now David completed the family.

My mother was under the doctor and I often heard mention of a Doctor Glen that was from Wellfield Surgery on Oldham Road in Rochdale. He used to attend to my mother's medical problems.

When she was a younger girl,

Joyce suffered with bronchitis and she had treatment for this. She ate spoonfuls of malt.

My parents decided that they needed more help looking after the children so they moved house from Watkin Street to 40 Howard Street, Rochdale. This was so they could live nearer to Joyce's parents so that they could help them to look after the children.

Chapter Four: The Observant Child

We now lived across the road from our grandparents Ethel and John Mitchell, who lived at 4 Leamington Street Rochdale. Later I would wonder why we did not have a bathroom but my grandparents did have one!

I was told that I often observed things that went on in my surroundings as I was a very observant child. My father said that when I was in my pram my eyes were darting all over the place, taking in information and interested in everything.

I observed things that went on around me and these things had a deep influence upon me and gave an insight into the thoughts and feelings of other people even if I was not talking directly to them. For this reason, I have many memories from my childhood, some are happy and a lot of them are sad.

Our house at 40 Howard Street had two rooms upstairs. This was two bedrooms and no bathroom.

It had two rooms downstairs, which consisted of the living room and the kitchen. The kitchen comprised a wooden clothes rack that hung above our heads.

It also had a kitchenette which was considered modern furniture at the time. Ours was yellow in colour. It comprised frosted glass cupboard doors and a worktop. It had three drawers in which to put kitchen utensils.

The kitchen also had built in drawers in one corner of the room and there were five of these and they went all of the way up to the ceiling.

The house had a back yard with an outside toilet.

Every morning Geoffrey left 2s and 6d for the housekeeping. He would leave it on the kitchen table for my mother to do the housekeeping for a day.

So when she'd dropped us off at school she went shopping for our tea. Our father always insisted upon eating brown wholemeal bread because of the fibre content and also because it tasted better than white bread, he said. Anne always liked white bread best for cucumber sandwiches.

Mother would go to Yorkshire Street in Rochdale town centre to buy the bread. She went to a shop called Bon bons which was a bakers shop and had a café upstairs. She put on her black zip-up ankle boots and off she would go after she sent us off to school.

The sides of the yard were unkempt, with grey slate slabs which acted as a fence. They were fastened together with massive round screws,

Here in this yard my brother and sister and I would play for hours.

Here is where I felt safe and secure and here is where I belonged.

Anne and I were allowed to go out of the yard and sometimes we played on the waste ground that is now known as Falinge flats.

The year was 1961 and we were growing up fast.

I remember several of the neighbours' children were our friends and playmates.

Two doors away in another terraced house lived my friend Deborah Hudson with her parents and three sisters Kelly, Rebecca and Belinda and then next door to them lived their grandmother Vera, a tall red-headed woman.

Her son lived with her, his name was Michael Corrigan. Whenever there was any trouble or upset on the street Michael Corrigan was always involved in it.

He was also cruel to animals. Once he wanted me to go into his back yard so that he could show me his hamster.

The poor animal had been tied to a wheel and he was spinning it round and round.

I told his mother about it and he had to stop doing it.

It is said that some criminals start off in life by being cruel to animals when they are children and I know that Michael Corrigan later ended up in trouble with the police and went to a borstal, which is a boys' house of correction.

Then there was Wendy Copestick, who lived beside us. Her house was a garden-fronted terrace with a back yard.

Once she collected some frogs from the pond in Falinge Park and they hatched in her back yard. They were jumping everywhere.

They were the tiniest frogs ever and we all loved to see them jumping. Of course, it was cruel really to have taken them away from their natural habitat, which was Falinge Park pond.

Some of them she had swimming in a bowl because they were still tadpoles.

Across the road lived Gillian Henshaw with her parents and her older brother Brian; years later he was killed in a motorbike accident and left his poor mother devastated.

On the corner was a toffee shop, or should I say a shop that sold toffees. The owner of the shop was called Mrs Cockroft.

On the front door of the shop it said, 'The place to buy 10001 dry foam and 10001 other good things.'

I went in the shop as a young child. I used to wander all over by myself as there was not much traffic in those days, my sister Anne and I began to get very adventurous and we would explore several places that were further and further away from home. Our mother was looking after our baby brother David.

Mrs Cockcroft would say, "Hello Sandra, what can I do for you today?"

I'd say, "Hello Mrs Cockcroft, could I see the penny tray please?"

Mrs Mabel Cockcroft, a small stout woman with tight black curls in her hair, would pull the penny tray from behind the counter.

On it were displayed the most scrumptious sweets, large white chocolate mice, penny bubble gum and lollipops.

I chose my twopence worth of sweets, and then returned to my house across the road, the house at number 40 with its radiant red front door with a white border running all the way around it with its characteristic Yale lock. Here I was safe and my surroundings were familiar to me.

At the end house at Leamington Street lived the two Mrs Wards. Miss Ward was the sister-in-law of Mrs Nellie Ward because Mrs Ward had married Miss Ward's brother. He had lived at the house with Nellie before he died of old age and natural causes. Miss Ward had apparently lived with them both. Grandma often stopped and chatted to them over their garden gate. Nellie was about ninety and her sister-in-law was around eighty. I never knew Miss Ward's Christian name!

Mrs Ward had had no children of her own and was now a widow. Her sister-in-law had become an old maid.

Mrs and Miss Ward lived at number 10 Leamington Street.

Our family on Grandma's side had special connections with the two 'Mrs Wards' as we used to call them. I can honestly say that these two old ladies were two of the nicest people that I have ever met in my life. They felt like our relations. Grandma said they had lived in their house at Leamington Street before she moved into her house at no. 4 and that they had watched my mother Joyce grow up.

When I was six years old my parents bought me a Sindy doll for my birthday. The Sindy doll was not as glamorous as a Barbie doll but she was still a fashion doll and I loved her to bits! I had a birthday party to celebrate being six.

The party took place in the kitchen of our house. The children that came to my party were the neighbours' children, who were more or less the same age as me, like Deborah Hudson from next door but one.

One girl knocked on our red front door and my father answered it and in came Anne Bancroft from across the street. She was in the same year as me at Cronkeyshaw Primary School.

She had brought me a colouring book. I put it into the bottom kitchen drawer. The drawers were large and painted yellow. They were built in drawers and they went right up to the ceiling.

Then there was another knock at the door. In came Gillian Henshaw from across the road. She handed me exactly the same colouring book! I did not want to upset either of the two girls by telling them that they each bought me the same identical colouring book so I hid this second colouring book in the bottom yellow drawer as well!

We played pass the parcel and passed the parcel around the kitchen table. The prize was a packet of wax crayons.

I had a lovely birthday cake and six candles. I stood on a kitchen chair and blew out the candles as everyone sang 'Happy Birthday' to me and as soon as I blew out all the candles the electric light over our heads went out.

Could this be an omen of things to come?

Our father went for Christmas in a big way and every year he decorated the house with paper chains which we all helped him to make. He also put up trimmings right across the ceiling.

We had a plastic Christmas tree. It was green in colour to represent a fir tree. Our father said it was a Canadian pine Christmas tree which he had bought especially because it had been imported from Canada. He liked to reminisce about the time he had spent in Canada whilst he was in the army.

Every Christmas we would find presents in a pillow case at the end of our beds.

On Christmas Day in 1963 I had a bride doll for Christmas. It had lovely teeth at the front as well as wearing a beautiful white bride dress. Anne had a Betta Bilda to make little houses with plastic bricks. David found a Meccano in his Christmas pillow case with a super ball as a stocking filler. It was the size of a golf ball. He had hours of fun playing with his super ball. It bounced as high as the houses!

It kept going into the neighbour's yard and Anne kept having to run and retrieve it, which she was not happy about!

One Saturday, when our father was out, Michael Corrigan climbed up onto our toilet roof and was throwing stones at our kitchen window. Our mother Joyce did not know what to do and Anne had to run over the road to fetch Grandad to get him down from our toilet roof and go back to his own house.

One year at school I made the Mrs Wards a Christmas present. It was a 2 lb bag of sugar wrapped in silver foil. Such a practical idea and they loved it when I gave it them for Christmas!

Grandma and Grandad Mitchell had lived at number 4 Leamington Street for years. Grandma later told me that she loved the house and had never wanted to leave.

Grandma had worked on the garden and it had a lovely green lawn and flower beds of all her favourite flowers. As children we loved playing on the lawn with games such as leap frog and it was safer to play on softer ground because we only had a back yard to play in but we were very happy as children with our mother Joyce as our main carer.

Every Sunday we would go across the street to Grandma's house for our weekly bath.

This is because we did not have a bathroom at Howard Street.

This was always a time of fun.

We both went in the bath together at the same time.

David would go in the tin baby bath and Mother would bath him in the kitchen.

He would slap his hand into the water and the soapy suds would spill over the side of the bath until the floor was wet. David was three years old back then.

Chapter Five: Clyde Street

Around this time our father Geoffrey took us on a family trip to London.

We went on several trips as children and each one educated us more, because this is what travel does.

We set off, our family of five. That was our father, our mother and us three children on a trip to London. Our dad said we were going to visit the Tower of London.

We went on the train to London. In those days the trains had corridors with carriages running off them.

People would sometimes open the window of the corridors if they were hot and wanted some air and sometimes an idiot would stick their head right out of the window and get hit by a train coming from the opposite direction. Thank God I never witnessed this myself but I have heard of it.

We went on an outing to Belle Vue Zoo and we had a ride on an elephant.

There was a huge basket on the elephant's back that contained several small chairs that the children were seated on and these were evenly spaced on both sides of the elephant's back.

I must confess that I found this ride a little frightening. These rides have now been banned because of animal cruelty.

Grandad John Mitchell occasionally took us to visit his mother, who was our great-grand mother.

She was our grandad's mother and I consider that we were very lucky to have met her. We did not visit her very often, probably only once every six months. Grandad said that she was very sad because she had lost her husband Joseph and she was a widow. She went into deeper mourning after the death of our mother. Joyce had been her granddaughter and when John and Ethel my grandparents had first got married they lived with Nancy and her husband Joseph at 23 Clyde Street at Newbold in Rochdale and Joyce had been born in this very house and Nancy had helped at her birth by bringing hot water and towels for the midwife.

We called her our `great-grandma in Clyde Street.'

Her name was Nancy Elisabeth Strand before she married Joseph Mitchell in 1904.

She was born in 1880 and gave birth to our Grandad John in 1904 when she was twenty-four years old. Through family research I found out that she, too, was pregnant with my grandad when she got married.

Our great-grandmother dressed in skirts and dresses that were maxi length. This meant that they were down to the floor. She always wore black cotton skirts and dresses. I never saw her in any other colour. When she went out she wore a dark shawl over her head.

Going to visit our great-grandmother was a fascinating experience.

Like our grandfather Major Schofield she had a Victorian fire range which was an open fire for a cooker and a large metal cupboard at the side of the range to keep food warm.

She always prepared ham teacakes for us to eat. This food always reminds me of my great-grandmother.

When we visited her she would stare at me in rather a stern manner as if she was completely weighing me up and at times I found it rather intimidating.

I think this was her way of controlling my behaviour and as she had lived in Victorian times she was the oldest person that I ever knew because she was even older than my grandparents!

Her house at 23 Clyde Street was a terraced house with no front garden.

Her house had no bathroom and she did not have a backyard with a toilet. She shared a toilet with the neighbours. Outside her back door was a communal area rather than a backyard.

If we needed to use the toilet whilst we were visiting her we were shown a tin bucket that was behind a curtain in the kitchen. This curtain and bucket were under the kitchen sink.

The bucket contained disinfectant. This was to counteract the smell of urine in the bucket. Each day she emptied the bucket of urine into the communal toilet that she shared with the neighbours at the back of her house.

Her husband Joseph Mitchell had died before I was born. He had died just after the birth of my older sister Anne, when she was eight weeks old, in July 1956. He was eighty years old when he died, so he must have been born in 1876 which made him four years older than his wife.

So Nancy Elisabeth was a widow who now lived alone, she was very strict in everything that she said and did because she had lived and been born during the Victorian era.

Nancy Elisabeth was born in 1880 and I feel privileged to have known her.

When twilight came and daylight started to fade she would light the gas light with a match.

The gas light hung above our heads in the living room. We were never allowed to go out of the living room into the kitchen space. Here there would be a kitchen sink. The open fire was used as the cooker and she did not have a fridge or a washing machine.

She did all her clothes washing by hand and hung them outside the back door in the communal area.

Like our Grandad Schofield she hung out her washing using dolly pegs and a rope like a washing line. She was a very strict lady and we always sat quietly when visiting her.

Upstairs there was one bedroom and no bathroom.

There was a coal fire with an oven at the side of it.

When she cooked anything the pan went straight on the fire and then kept warm in the oven at the side which had become hot from the heat off the fire.

The last time I saw her we had gone to see her to tell her that we were going to live in an orphanage in Derbyshire.

She had been heartbroken when our mother Joyce died as this had been her granddaughter who had been born at her house in Clyde Street.

When we were leaving she said to us, "Take these purses because I might never see you again."

And she gave Anne and I identical white purses that were embroidered with pearls. She gave David a little yellow teddy.

Our great-grandma in Clyde Street died in 1966 at the age of eighty-six years.

Later, Grandad John Mitchell told me that he went to visit her one Sunday and she told him that she felt unwell and had pains in her chest. She had said that she did not want to see a doctor so Grandad had to adhere to her wishes. Grandad said he was going home for his tea and our great-grandma said, "Don't go this is the last time that you will ever see me," so Grandad stayed with her and a few hours later she collapsed and died.

We did not attend our great-grandmother's funeral because we were away in Derbyshire.

She is buried in the same grave as my mother Joyce in Rochdale Cemetery.

Also in the grave is Joseph Mitchell my great-great-grandfather, who was buried in 1890.

When my mother died my grandfather John visited her grave every week. As time went on this dwindled to once a month and then birthdays and Christmas. As time is a great healer our grandfather did not feel the need to visit the grave as much as time went on. As Christians we believe that her spirit has been lifted to a higher life.

Eventually after about ten years he visited the grave only at Christmas.

As adults we visited our mother's grave on Mother's Day and at Christmas.

Chapter Six: The Wedding

Our parents announced that they were leaving us in the house and that they were going to attend a wedding. It was the wedding of my mother's brother Jack Mitchell, who was our uncle.

He was marrying a woman called Yvonne, who was apparently having his baby.

Our father said to expect a babysitter to arrive in ten minutes. They were going to leave the front door ajar so that she could come in.

"Who is it that is coming?" asked Anne. Our father said that he did not know. He said that he had rung a babysitting agency out of the newspaper. This was the done thing in those days.

It would be someone who was qualified to look after children.

So our parents went out and left us in the house. Anne had an idea to make the kitchen floor into a skating rink.

She began filling a bucket full of water. When it was full, she poured it onto the stone kitchen floor. Then she squirted fairy liquid onto the floor.

So I followed suit and started to fill the bucket up as well. David said we had to stop doing it.

I was filling a bucket of cold water and David said not to pour it onto the floor but I did and then Anne did another bucket and added the Fairy liquid.

David did not like it. Anne and I were skating up and down the kitchen.

Then it was my turn to fill another bucket of water. I had filled it about half way when David appeared at the side of the sink complaining about what we were doing so I poured some water on him out of the bucket.

When the babysitter finally arrived, they had a lot of cleaning up to do.

Chapter Seven: Gathering Strength

One day my mother was furious about something. She had been having an argument with my father.

I had been playing in the back yard with a pram that was made out of tin and it had a tin hood that would not go up and down because it was made of tin!

"Right! Get your coats," our mother shouted. It was unusual to hear her as upset as this. I ran into the house and grabbed my coat from behind the kitchen door. Anne appeared from upstairs where she had been playing with her Lego set.

David had been at the kitchen table trying to fathom his Meccano set and now our mother was helping him on with his coat.

"Where are we going, Mummy?" he enquired.

"Never mind," replied our mother, now intent on rounding up her chickens, which was us three children and getting out of the house as quickly as possible.

We all went out of the back door, our mother holding onto young David's hand whilst Anne and I ran ahead.

We went out of the back yard turning right at the end of the alley and past the bollard onto Howard Street then turned to go up the street.

"Go to Grandma's front door," commanded our mother, so we ran ahead, Anne and I, and turned left into Leamington Street and waited for our mother to catch up. She was still holding onto David's hand.

Together now we marched up Leamington Street to our grandmother's gate. I observed that my mother was crying.

We opened Grandma's fancy front gate and went into the front garden.

Our mother rang the bell and we waited for Grandma to answer the door.

Our mother blurted, "I'm leaving him this time."

We waited for an answer and then she rang the doorbell again.

"They must be out. We'll wait here for a while."

We played at leap frog though I knew something was wrong with my saint-like mother.

I thought, "Please answer the door, Grandma. Mummy is so upset."

Eventually she gave up and said she was going back home. She went back down Leamington Street, turned right past Mrs

Cockroft's shop, then left into Howard Street. We crossed the road to our familiar house at number 40 with its red door with a white border and our darling mother let herself in by opening the Yale lock which was too high on the door for me to reach.

We had no choice but to return but thought she might go back when our grandparents returned but she never attempted this again.

Shortly after this incident I recall I was in the kitchen of the house at 40 Howard Street when my father was shouting at my mother about something. My mother was standing at the kitchen sink.

I was looking at her poor crying face when my father threw a wet dishcloth right into her face.

These incidents always brought me out of my happy play mode into a few moments of horror.

One Sunday in the early evening I was sitting in our living room on the green armchair watching our black and white television. Our mother Joyce was not in the house, she had gone to visit our grandparents who lived across the road. The rest of the family were seated on the green settee.

I heard Grandma's voice.

"We have had to send for an ambulance for our Joyce, she is not well. All her legs are puffed up like a balloon."

Immediately we all jumped to our feet and put on our shoes, or whatever it was we needed to put on, to be able to follow our grandmother back over the road. As usual she was wearing a silk scarf around her head. I observed this because Grandma hardly ever went out at all.

Within seconds we had arrived at our mother's bedside.

"Where is she, Grandma?" Anne had asked as we were charging over the road.

"She's in Grandad's bed," came the reply.

We were both at the house before Grandma and as the door was open we ran straight up the stairs.

The scene that met me will be with me for the rest of my life.

Our mother was in bed covered by Grandad's red eiderdown.

David, who had earlier gone to visit Grandma with our mother was playing with a train set on the floor. The little electric train went round and round the track. It was making me dizzy but I did not speak, I just observed everything.

I stood in the room and now observed everything. Anne threw herself on our mother.

"Mummy, don't go into hospital," she wailed. "You might not come home again."

Straight away I heard strange voices were in the house and coming up the stairs.

"She's in the front bedroom," cried our grandmother.

An ambulance man came into the bedroom and Grandma came running in behind him.

"What's the matter, love?" he asked our mother, to which she replied, "I'm all swelled up."

The ambulance man began to examine our mother. After a few minutes he said, "Your stomach is swollen but you're not pregnant, it's a stomach full of water."

"My legs are swollen too," retorted our mother.

Grandma announced that our mother had not been to the toilet in order to pass water for several hours and seemed unable to do so.

The ambulance man said it sounded like her kidneys and that she would have to go into hospital.

Once again Anne flung herself over our mother.

"Please don't go into hospital," she begged. "You might never come back."

She walks in beauty
She walks in beauty like the night of cloudless climes
And starry skies
And all that's best of dark and bright
Meet in her aspect and her eyes
Thus mellowed to the tender light
Which heaven to gaudy day denies
One shade the more, one ray the less
Had half impaired the nameless grace
Which weaves in every raven stress
Or softly lightens o'er her face;
When thoughts serenely sweet express
How pure, how dear their dwelling place

Chapter Eight: The Day the Sky Fell Down

The following Thursday, we three children woke up to an eerie silence, we had slept longer than usual and our dad was not in the house, never before had we awoken to find neither of our parents in the house.

We stood at the top of the stairs wondering what to do. We heard a light tapping at the back door and we could hear our grandma's voice.

"Come and open the door," she said.

We all three went downstairs, opening the stair door as we went.

We could see our grandma's grey face at the window surrounded by a pale blue scarf.

Anne had to pull a kitchen dining chair over to the door to open it. She started to pull back the giant steel bar and as I stood observing the scene the whole ambience went into slow motion.

The door opened and there stood our grandma looking solemn and serious. She wore a pale blue raincoat which matched her scarf.

"Can you all get dressed and come with me," was the appeal.

Straight away we scrambled into our clothes that were in the kitchen. I helped David on with his shoes and off we went in the blink of an eye, trudging the journey across the street to Grandma's house in total silence.

We turned round like clockwork statues to see Grandma crying on Mrs Ward's shoulder.

Anne said to me, "Our mother has died."

I did not dare to speak as I could not possibly believe it even for one second. I could not let this thought enter my head and it must be kept away at all cost.

When Grandma caught up with us Anne asked, "Our mum has died, hasn't she?" to which our grandma replied, "Yes."

We carried on walking towards Grandma's house as if it were a nightmare from which we wished to wake up from.

Once in the house, entering through the kitchen door Anne fell to her knees on the floor. She said later that the black and white tiles on the kitchen lino had begun to move and the squares were going into each other. She had to fall on her knees in order to steady herself.

The whole household was in a state of absolute shock. Grandad had gone a grey colour and he looked like he thought that it was the end of the world.

He said, "A young nurse called here this morning. She said that she had been working on the night shift at Birch Hill Hospital and that she had been nursing our mother in the night but she had passed away and the doctor that was there was unable to save her."

My grandad said to the nurse, "Did Joyce say any last words?"

He said that the nurse had replied that our mother had said, "Hello, Grandad", just before she died.

Grandad said she was talking about his father Joseph Mitchell who had died in 1956, just two months after my older sister Anne had been born. Joyce had been close to her grandad whilst she was growing up.

A couple of days after this, Grandad said he wanted her to be buried with her grandfather Joseph Mitchell in Rochdale cemetery.

David did not understand what it all meant. He could not take it in. He was five years old.

I coped by pretending it was not true and that some kind of a mistake had been made.

When I went to bed I dreamed about her. She was sat on the arm of the green three-seater settee as she often used to do.

I turned to her and said, "You're not dead, Mummy."

She looked at me and said, "Am I not?" as if she did not know whether she was dead or not. It was as if in my dream that she needed it confirming.

Our mother's body was brought to Grandma's house where we were now all staying.

Her coffin was laid out in the front room of Grandma's house. The door to the room was firmly closed and the windows had the curtains closed.

Children were not allowed to enter the room. At the window to the room which was at the front of the house the curtains were closed. The whole house engaged into a total solemnness.

The whole street was quiet, as everyone seemed to know a young woman of thirty-seven years old had died and left three small children aged five, seven and nine years old.

We stayed at Grandma's house for a few days and after the funeral we returned to live with our father for a time but we never returned to Cronkeyshaw Primary school.

Our devoted and darling mother had died on 2nd September during the school holidays in 1965.

We were bought black clothes to wear for the funeral. Anne had a black duffle coat and

David and I each had a black gaberdine rain coat.

I often wondered why Anne had a duffle coat which had been imported from Belgium, according to the man in the shop. I had to make do with a gaberdine rain coat the same as David. Also, David and I had lace up black leather shoes and Anne's were a T-bar, a much more modern shoe.

I did not complain, I just carried on doing as I was told. As the middle child I tried to please everyone. I was in the position of being neither the oldest or the youngest child.

On the day of the funeral, we scrambled into the hearse. My father had seated himself at the most convenient seat near the door of the hearse.

I sat opposite him and stared at him. I observed that he was crying crocodile tears. He was pretending to cry. It occurred to me that I had never seen him crying before. I realised when I was older that this was a show for Grandma and Grandad, he was afraid of them.

We watched our mother's coffin going into the earth and I read the gold plaque on the coffin. It said:

Joyce Schofield nee Mitchell born
13/6/1928 died 2nd September 1965

I read it but the words would not really sink in. And I looked up and observed that my aunty Yvonne was gazing right at me with an incredible stare. I could not understand this but I observed it.

After the funeral, the entourage went to a café at the bottom of Yorkshire Street in Rochdale. It was called Bon bons café. This was a café above the baker's shop where my mother shopped for bread.

We all climbed the steps to Bon bon café.

All week I had been waiting for Mummy to come home and I could wake up from this horrible nightmare. I waited and waited and prayed so hard for her to come home.

Now I had seen the writing on the coffin as the rope lowered the precious cargo into its resting place. She was buried next to her grandad Joseph Mitchell.

When we arrived at the top of the steps of Bon bons café we were shown to our tables.

I sat down next to my father and my siblings surrounded the table. I thanked God for my brother and sister at that moment.

Then the most enormous bowl of chicken soup was placed in front of me by a waitress.

It felt as though I had been served the soup in a washing up bowl. I moved the soup this way and that and the soup went up and down like the waves of the sea. I took one tablespoonful of the soup and put it in my mouth.

The soup was in front of me like an abyss that I might just drown in.

Then there was laughter. It was a man's laugh. He was laughing and laughing and laughing.

It was my great-uncle Jim that was laughing. I recognised his voice now. I didn't know what he was laughing about but years later I realised he must have felt embarrassed at the situation.

After this we lived at my grandparents' house again. There was a dispute going on between my father and my grandparents. They said Geoffrey our father was not allowed to have any contact with us.

Our grandparents were blaming our father for the death of our mother. They said her life had been too hard.

What did they mean? Was it because she had had three children? Was it because she never got enough to eat? Was it because she hardly ever had any luxury? Was it because she had suffered badly with her health?

However, we never went back to Cronkeyshaw Primary School and our father announced that we were to be sent to an orphanage.

Anne pleaded with our father not to send us to an orphanage. She offered to do all the household chores during her spare time. Our father said that she was too young to do this. He would not be persuaded to change his mind.

Grandma had said that there were too many of us to live at her house permanently. Even if we had gone there, Grandma said that Geoffrey would not be allowed in the house and she preferred never to see him again.

Our father still worked on the railway at Rochdale station. He worked as a clerk in the office there and he had been making enquiries about sending us to an orphanage. He would be able to send us to a railway home in Derbyshire.

At the time he said he wanted contact with us and Grandma was refusing to let him see us. By sending us to an orphanage he said he would get contact with us at weekends. He was appearing to be a very selfish man. We as children felt helpless about our own fate.

My skin broke out very badly and the family doctor was sent for. He said I needed to go for a spell in hospital.

Our father Geoffrey came to collect Anne and David and he took them to an orphanage.

The orphanage was in Derbyshire and it was called St Christopher's Home for Orphaned Children at Ashgate in Derbyshire.

So now I stayed at Grandma's having treatment for my eczema whilst my brother and sister went to an orphanage.

Chapter Nine: Booth Hall Hospital

I went into hospital about a week before Christmas in 1965. Grandma took me and left me there. I was in my own cubicle. This was called being in isolation. I was a very sociable child so did not stay in this room for very long.

At first the nurse covered me in a greasy ointment and covered me in bandages from head to foot.

There were other children in all of the other cubicles. Some of them were walking about in the corridor outside the cubicles.

One girl who must have been about four years old was getting a lot of attention from the nurses, I observed.

The little girl's name was Queenie. She had very bad asthma and bronchitis. Her voice was very hoarse and she could not get her breath properly. In her room was an oxygen tent and when she went to bed she was given a constant stream of oxygen.

I sat in the corridor a lot. As usual I observed what was going on around me. One girl had her mother visit her and I knew that my mother was not coming to see me in the hospital but I dared not tell anyone why she was not coming in case it came true.

The nurse came around with a trolley serving drinks and biscuits. Every evening at about 7 p.m. I waited for her arrival. She gave me a drink of orange in a steel cup. The cup felt comforting, it was a billy boiler. Now every time I see a steel cup it reminds me of the committed and hard-working nurses at Booth Hall Hospital.

The next day Grandma and Grandad came to see me in the hospital at visiting time. Grandma had a basket from which she pulled out some apples and oranges for me. The nurse brought a fruit bowl and placed them on my locker.

"I'm covered in bandages, Grandma," I said. "I've got them on my arms and legs."

Grandad said, "Well, let's hope they get you right." He always spoke in a Lancashire dialect.

The doctor came to speak with my grandparents.

"You have to keep on top of eczema as it is very dry skin that needs to be covered in greasy ointment."

They both left after about thirty minutes.

"We'll have to get t'bus, Etu."

This was his pet name for Grandma as her name was Ethel.

They came to see me only once because they had to catch four buses because they did not have a car and they could not drive and were dependent on public transport.

Every day my skin was greased and covered in bandages by the nurse. I had cotton gloves on my hands. The bandages were a kind of muslin.

After about a week it was much improved.

A nurse said, "There's a Christmas party tomorrow and since you are well enough to go home, you can go to the Christmas party if you like."

I said I would go to the party and the next day a nurse brought me a red dressing gown to attend the party.

The children that were soon going home set off to the Christmas party, which was on another ward. We were told that if we went we would probably be on the telly because the television crew came to Booth Hall Hospital every year to visit the children and it was televised on Christmas day.

When we arrived at the ward there were some children in bed and some sat on chairs. I was one of the children sitting on chairs. I was aware there was a television camera filming the children and I spotted a man that I had seen on the telly. His name was Leslie Crowther, a well-known TV personality.

As I sat on the chair I could sense that the camera had come right up to my face. Then Lesley Crowther gave me a present.

On Christmas Day I was watching the television at Grandma's house looking out for myself on the telly. After a while I realised I was watching the wrong channel!

Immediately Grandad turned the channel over and the right programme had just finished.

I began to wonder if I had been on the telly at all.

One day after the Christmas holidays Grandma arrived back from the corner shop and declared, "Sandra, Mrs Cockroft has seen you on the telly!"

Soon it was time for me to join my two siblings in Derbyshire. I would have liked to stay longer at my grandparents' house but I knew it was right for me to join them. They needed my strength.

My father Geoffrey collected me from my grandparents' house to take me to Derbyshire. My skin was now much improved and I had a moisturiser to apply twice a day, which I did in the morning and the evening.

Chapter Ten: St Christopher's: A Chateau Home

We travelled on a train to Derbyshire. It was one of the old type of trains that had carriages and a corridor going right through the train and past all of the carriages. The journey took about an hour.

"How far is it to Derbyshire?" I enquired.

"It's a hundred miles," replied my father.

Readers may be horrified to read this and think how awful that her father is taking her to an orphanage and leaving her there, but in those days, everything was an adventure to me and I was extremely resilient. I looked forward to seeing my brother and sister again. It was now three months since they went to the orphanage without me. I had had no contact with them at all during this time.

When my father and I emerged from the train, my siblings were on the platform waiting for me.

As soon as I saw them I went up to them because they were both standing still and looking at me in disbelief as if they could not believe I was there.

“Look,” I said whilst holding up my hands. “My eczema has gone now!”

They both appeared very anxious, especially David, as if they thought that I had deliberately stayed away and I realised they had lost some trust in me during these three months apart and it was going to take some time to get the trust back.

Miss Band took us to our destination in her car. I was being driven into strange new territory and a new chapter of my life was about to begin. I was aware of being driven up a very long driveway to an enormous building

We went in through some doors at the side of the building and I followed Miss Band into what was known as the day room. At once a crowd of children gathered around me. Another member of staff had been waiting to try a coat on me. It was an orange coat that had belonged to another child but they had grown out of it, the member of staff said. I tried it on and it was a perfect fit. Strange faces stood around me as if assessing their new playmate. I felt a little afraid but also a little excited as I embarked on another adventure. The coat was bright and perfect and I loved it.

Our father Geoffrey left us all there and for the next few months he would visit us every

Sunday and enjoy a Sunday lunch cooked by the kitchen staff at the orphanage.

'St Christopher's Home for Orphaned Children' was the sign at the bottom of the driveway. There were two driveways to the building. One was the east wing and the other one was known as the west wing and it was in the style that is known as a chateau design, which originally comes from France.

On entering through the east wing entrance door, the office was on the left. This was Miss Priestman's office.

The next room was the day room, which was designed for leisure activities. The children were aged from three to sixteen years old.

Further along the corridor was the other entrance door. This entrance door contained a letter box where some of the older children checked if they had any mail. Any mail for the home also came through this letter box.

The whole home had a lot of dark corridors with rooms leading off them. There was a corridor that led straight from the day room to another corridor. Turn left here and there was the dining room where all the children had their meals on long tables. Past the dining room and there were some winding stairs. At the top of these on the left was a bathroom. Here there was a line of baths that stood higher than the floor and freestanding on four legs. This is where the children would take a bath.

Then opposite the stairs there was a corridor that led straight on and another one that turned to the left on the landing. The first room straight on the left was the girls' dormitory. Further on up the corridor was the sewing room where an old lady sewed the children's clothes.

Opposite the girls' dormitory there was a chapel where the children would sing hymns and pray on Sundays.

I slept in the girls' dormitory. My bed was the one nearest to the door and Anne slept in the next bed to me. Everyone had a small wardrobe next to their bed. The beds were all in a line on each side of the wall.

David slept in the boys' dormitory and had been crying in the night. Anne said she had to go and give him a cuddle every night.

After I arrived at the orphanage David settled down to sleep at night and Anne was no longer sent for. David now had my strength that I gave him and my three month absence was soon forgotten about. It seemed that I had taken on a maternal role for David without even realising it.

David attended an all-boys school called Ashgate School for Boys. This was very close to the orphanage and he set off to school every morning with Anne and myself. Anne and I attended Ashgate School for Girls and this was next door. All the children had breakfast in the dining room and then made their way to school. The staff were very caring.

I started to look upon my time at the orphanage as an adventure. I suppose I must have been very resilient because I was only a child.

I remember standing in a school yard waiting to go into the school. Anne had gone to her class, a girl in front of me said, “Hello, you’re new here, aren’t you?”

I said “yes”, I’d only just started at the school that day.

“Oh well, I am Pamela and guess what my second name is?”

“I don’t know.”

“My second name is ‘Payne.’ Do you know when you get a pain?”

“Yes.”

“Well, my second name is Payne and it sounds the same as when you have a pain!”

Pamela was sure to show me the ropes but the sight of the school teacher made me rather nervous.

The teacher was tall and round and wore a pair of spectacles on the end of her pointed nose. She wore her dark hair in a high bun that stood on the top of her head.

During my time in this school, I don't think I did very well in any subject at all.

One morning I remember coming out of the orphanage in order to go to the school which was in fact practically next door but I found that I could not walk down the driveway because it was covered in ice so I sat down on my bottom and slid down it until I had got past the slope on the driveway and then I stood up and then I walked the rest of the way to the school. I was a bit wet and just had to dry off!

On Saturdays the children could relax and play in the grounds of the orphanage. There were some pet guinea pigs that were kept in cages in the grounds and we liked to look at these. Some of the children were allotted to look after them. We played with the guinea pigs on Saturdays. There were also some swings for the children play on.

On Saturdays Anne and David and I would swing on them and practise singing songs such as *A World of their Own* by The Seekers.

On Saturdays, the children would queue up in the day room for our pocket money. We all got 6d each. Miss Band would give each child their sixpence out of a cash tin and then mark their name off in a book as having received their spending money. Most of the children spent their pocket money on sweets.

The big wooden gates at the back of the orphanage would open and the children flooded out to race to the sweet shop which was on the corner at the bottom of the road.

The threat of traffic accidents was much less in those days because not many people had a car.

The children moved around freely when not in the orphanage grounds and we were not frightened of strangers and hardly anyone spoke to us anyway, apart from the orphanage staff of course. I began to feel a connection with the other children there. We all had no mother and we had to try and make the most of it. I began to realise that I may not see my mother again in this life but my Christian faith helped me to pull through and I felt all the children pulled together like one big family, and we supported each other.

I began to settle into life at the orphanage. I learned to ride a two-wheeler push bike. Before I went to the orphanage I could only ride a three-wheeler push bike which actually belonged to the neighbour. "It's a matter of keeping your balance," said my friend Susan Cadbury, who was one of the orphans. I played out in the grounds with her and several of the others.

The orphanage had its own swimming pool and I had never been to the swimming baths before.

On Saturday afternoons the children went in the swimming pool. It was always under the supervision of the orphanage staff.

I remember when I went into the pool for the first time I wore a swimming costume made of a bubbly material in a red colour. I had never seen or felt this material before and I really liked it. I also wore a white rubber swimming hat. This blocked out a lot of sound. I went into the pool by going down the steps and then reaching the floor of the shallow end, holding onto the bar at the side of the pool. The smell of the chlorine hit me.

Holding up my head I was only just tall enough to stand up in the shallow end. I walked along with the other non-swimmers, holding onto the silver bar that stretched all around the pool.

At the next swimming session the following Saturday, we were all given a board made out of polystyrene which kept us afloat whilst we hung onto it for dear life and paddled our legs and arms.

After a few lessons I got the hang of it and I could soon do a doggy paddle using both my arms and legs and I could swim a breadth across the pool!

My life became so full of adventure I rarely thought about my old life back in Rochdale. Anne said I was resilient but she said she longed to go back to Rochdale. David didn't care where he went as long as he was with his sisters.

Every Sunday our father Geoffrey would arrive to see us. The cook at the orphanage would cook him a Sunday roast dinner which he always ate eagerly. It was around three o'clock that he used to arrive and after his lunch he took us all out to Ashbourne Park. This was within walking distance of the orphanage.

On Sunday mornings we would attend the chapel in the orphanage and pray and sing hymns.

At the end of the service, I was fascinated by the chaplain putting out the altar candles with a pointed upside-down cup that was on a long stick.

Then we would all sing a song: *Fight the good fight with all thy might,* and other similar songs.

The long corridor leading to the boys' dormitory was rather creepy and dark. There was a box at the side of the corridor and I used to imagine that Herman Munster from *The Munsters* slept there and by day he crept around in the dark corridors of the home!

There was a sports day at the orphanage and I won the 100 metres race. I knew that I was very good at running short distances.

I remember one school day in 1966 Anne said she had been sent by Miss Band to collect a letter from the flower room. Anne, David and I were walking three abreast as Anne opened and read out the letter to us.

Dear children, it said, *I'm very sorry to have to tell you that your great-grandma in Clyde Street has died.*

All three of us started to cry and we cried all the way to school. The letter was signed from Grandad Mitchell. I do not think that we should have learned of our grandma's death in this way.

I remembered the little white clutch purses that she had given to Anne and I the last time that we had seen her and what she had said, that we might never see her again and I said to Anne and David, "She must have known that she was going to die. She was eighty-six years old."

I still miss her and think about her.

We did not attend the funeral as we were too far away. Besides, we had already attended the funeral of our mother and the death of one close relative and attending the funeral is enough for

There was also news that we had had a baby cousin born in 1966, his name was Christopher and he was a brother for our cousin Lynda.

Sometimes after school the three of us, Anne David and I, went on the swings that were at the orphanage and practised singing. We sang songs from The Seekers:

Close the door, light the light, we`re staying home tonight, far away from the bustle and the bright city light. Let them all fade away, just leave us alone and we'll live in a world of our own.

Anne and David practised a duet, *Somethin' Stupid* by Nancy and Frank Sinatra.

Soon Anne and I started attending the Brownies and we went every Tuesday evening. We had to salute the leader, who was known as Brown Owl, with two fingers like the sign of peace against our heads.

Every day at the orphanage seemed like fun and games and I can honestly say that I was happy there. I thought that there was no point in returning to a town where every child had a mother and I didn't have one. The children were all bonded by the fact that we were all in the same boat and that all our mothers had died.

As the year wore on it was soon time to start rehearsing for the annual Christmas play, and I was very pleased and completely un-surprised to hear that I had been selected as one of the actors to act in the Christmas play.

My part in the play was to be dressed in cottonwool and play the part of a snowball and I absolutely loved and looked forward to this.

Christmas 1966 and Mr Branch took us to a Christmas party. He was David's favourite member of staff because he always made everyone laugh. We called him Twiggy for short.

A twig is actually longer than a branch but it's all parts of a tree and pieces of wood!

Twiggy was actually disabled and could not walk properly. All the children loved him because he had a heart of gold and nothing was ever too much trouble for him.

We went to the party in a decorated room and eventually Father Christmas appeared and pulled presents for all the children from his big black sack! It was a great atmosphere for the kids.

I felt a connection with the other kids at the orphanage because we were all without a mother.

I wanted to stay with them and grow up with them at the orphanage. I thought that if we went back to Rochdale to live, we would be there without our mum.

I did not want to think about the sadness of this so I preferred to stay at St Christopher's. I was happy there. I had learned to swim and ride a bike. We were among our own kind (orphans), yet Anne wanted to return to Rochdale. Anne and I had both looked after David during our time at the orphanage.

Around this time on one of his Sunday visits our father Geoffrey came to see us and as usual he ate his Sunday lunch as we sat and waited for him. Suddenly he announced, "You will soon be leaving St Christopher's because I have found a new mother for you."

"Have you, Daddy?" said Anne, delighted.

Anne wanted to go back to Rochdale with him straight away; our father said he was to make further arrangements.

What he meant was he had not married her yet but was about to. Her name was Barbara.

I said, "I don't want a new mother."

David didn't seem to mind either way. He just wanted to be with his sisters.

I said, "I don't want a new mother and I want to stay here in the orphanage, I like it here."

Our father said I would have to do as I was told.

The thought of leaving made me sad as I acted my role as a snowball in the Christmas play, which was staged just a few days before Christmas 1966.

For my line I had to say, “Rather.”

The arrangements were made that we were to leave the orphanage just before Christmas 1966.

On the day of our departure, it was a Sunday and the children were sat at dining tables eating their Sunday lunch.

I went out of the door with my father and brother and sister and I looked back at the children in order to say goodbye to them. Every single one of them was looking down at their food, my heart went out to them and I wished at that moment that they were all coming with us.

Goodbye and farewell, my childhood friends, I have loved you all like my own family. I hope you all find the happiness that you deserve. Mon amie, it broke my heart to leave you.

Sandra's parents getting married

Sandra, age 6, with her Sindy doll

Her younger brother David, age 5

Sandra and brother David

Sandra with David and big sister Anne, holding her big dolly Walker, in the park

Sandra, Anne and David in their black funeral clothes

Sandra with Grandma Ethel and David

Sandra with Grandad John and David

Sandra and David on a boat ride

Taken in 1967 at Stanley Park in Blackpool, when Sandra and David started living with their Grandparents

Granddad John with Sandra age 10 and David age 8. David is still wearing short pants! Taken in Stanley Park

Sandra and David with a monkey in Blackpool

David is still wearing short pants in these photographs taken in 1970. Sandra is wearing a yellow blouse and wrap over skirt that she has made herself at school. Sandra age 12 and David age 10.

Becoming a teenager. Sandra age 13

David age 11 at Redbrook School

More photographs from holidays in Blackpool

Chapter Eleven: Living With a Stepmother

Our father Geoffrey had bought a new house whilst we were in the orphanage. It was called Ebor Mount in Whitworth in Rochdale. It was a very big and splendid house, with steps up to it at the front from the road.

Our father took us into the front room of the house. I saw some Christmas cards on the mantelpiece and went over to look at them. One said, 'To my wife' and I opened it and it said, 'Love from Geoffrey.'

I said, "Look at these cards, Anne and David," and we all looked at them.

The other card read, 'To my husband at Christmas,' and inside it said, 'Love from Barbara.'

Our father had disappeared upstairs. Suddenly a blonde woman came into the room, she must have come in the front door. We all looked at her.

"Where is he?" she asked. She was asking us where our father was. The meeting was awkward. Anne replied, "He's gone upstairs."

At this the woman who must have been Barbara went up the stairs after him.

Barbara was small, slim and blonde. She was ambitious and wanted to open her own shop.

She also smoked most of the time as if she thought it was rather trendy.

She said I was not allowed to play outside without wearing my coat. I soon made a few friends in the local area as I was rather an outdoors person by this time.

I preferred to make friends with other children as well as spend time with my siblings indoors.

Anne on the other hand, who had lots of friends whilst our mother was alive, now preferred to stay indoors and not attempt to make any friends. She had become introverted with the experience of losing our mother at such a young age.

We had an enormous skipping rope and two girls would keep the skipping rope going whilst children from the neighbourhood skipped within the rope and other children queued to take their turn.

Another game would be to place a tennis ball inside a silk stocking. We would borrow Barbara's silk stockings in order to play this game.

Then stand against a brick wall with legs apart. Bring the stocking with the ball inside until it bangs the wall at either side of your body and then when it gets swinging send it downwards and then upwards as well as side to side and at the same time sing this ditty:

My mother told me if I was goody that she would buy me a rubber dolly. My aunty told her I kissed a soldier now she won't buy me a rubber dolly!

Barbara wanted to teach us about fashionable clothes and she bought me a jumper dress, which was literally a jumper that had been knitted into a dress!

I liked wearing this dress and I started to think about fashion and clothes for girls my age.

I had a two-piece suit in dark green, it was a skirt and jacket set.

Soon Barbara started a greengrocer's shop.

It was across the street from where we lived at Whitworth near Rochdale.

She had fake green grass in the window of the shop. On this grass she carefully placed some lovely red tomatoes that looked as if they had been polished. She surrounded them with other fruits such as apples and oranges. It looked like a mouth-watering display that attracted many customers.

Barbara would smoke a lot and watch herself smoking in the mirror trying to make herself look alluring.

She would flirt with some of the male customers that came into the shop but I never told my father about this.

It was 1967 and now we were eleven, nine and seven years old.

We attended Tonacliffe School in Whitworth and went to school and back by ourselves.

Once a week we would have certain deliveries.

The Corona man would deliver ten bottles of Corona pop in different flavours.

We would have coal delivered for our open coal fire in the living room.

At night time our father would burn a paraffin lamp. The smell of it would infuse throughout the downstairs and upstairs rooms. It was not an unpleasant smell.

Ebor Mount had three bedrooms. Geoffrey and Barbara slept in the master bedroom that faced the front of the house.

There was a large family bathroom with a bath and I had never lived in a house that had a bath in it before!

Ebor Mount had a beautiful garden at the back of the house where a patch of rhubarb grew.

I loved it when Barbara stewed the rhubarb for our evening dessert and served it with custard.

It tasted delicious and I looked forward to tea when Barbara made this dessert!

Anne and I shared a bedroom and this was known as 'the girls' room' and David had the box room. It was big enough for him, now a seven-year-old boy growing up fast in 1967.

Sometimes Anne would read bedtime stories to me at night.

My favourite story was *The Little Match Girl*. It is a story of a poor little girl trying to sell matches, after a while she grows cold and cannot sell any of her matches.

The little match girl begins to strike the matches so that she can feel some heat and she sees glimpses of love in the flames. She sees her grandmother in the flame and goes to her.

For a short while things ran smoothly at Ebor Mount.

We sometimes played across the road at Healey Dell Nature Reserve, which is a wooded area surrounded with trees.

There is a river running through the nature reserve which is called the River Spodden.

It is a favourite spot for family picnics.

Sometimes we would go over to the nature reserve and take with us a large bottle of Corona pop and my favourite flavour was sarsaparilla.

We played there for hours at games like leap frog. This is when one person leans over pretending to be a frog. The other children leap over their back!

Our weekend outings that we had when our mother had been alive did not continue after we left Howard Street. These outings stayed as precious memories of our early childhood.

Now that we were older, we had to find our own interests at weekends.

I missed my grandparents and went to visit them regularly. I took a bus on the main road in Whitworth and it went down the dusty road and turned the corner until it reached my stop on Whitworth Road.

The bus was the old style, it had a driver and a conductor. There was a platform at the back of the bus where passengers boarded and dismounted the bus.

My grandparents Ethel and John were always so pleased to see me and I always felt loved by them.

Things went well for a while at Ebor Mount. Then it slowly started going wrong.

Barbara and our father Geoffrey were arguing quite a lot. Barbara said that she wanted to move house and own a shop.

She had seen a shop that she wanted on Primrose Street in Rochdale. It was a ‘live in’ grocers shop.

I was worried that Anne, David and I would have to go to different schools again in the middle of a school term as we were settling in at Tonacliffe School.

So it was not a good idea for us to move house.

Barbara was adamant that she wanted to move house. There were also problems within their marriage and they argued a lot.

Barbara complained that I was still refusing to call her “Mum” when I addressed her. I did not feel close enough to her, especially when she started saying that it was my fault that she and Geoffrey were always arguing. She said I was a constant reminder of my mother Joyce because I was ‘Joyce’s image’.

And so how could their marriage be a success when I was a constant reminder of his first wife? she said.

Anne liked Barbara a lot more than I did and she got along with her. David got along with her reasonably well, I thought.

We moved house and changed schools so this was more upheaval in our lives.

Then to my astonishment Anne failed her eleven-plus exam at school, so this meant that she could not go to grammar school as was intended, and now she would have to attend a comprehensive high school until she was fifteen. Fifteen was the school leaving age at the time.

Barbara started telling me that I could not have any food from the shop or from the living quarters of the house.

When I set off to school in the mornings I had to go without any breakfast and this was hard as I could not concentrate on my lessons at school. At the time, breakfast clubs in schools had not been invented.

I used to have school dinners which is a good thing as some days it was the only thing I ate all day.

Sometimes Barbara would make cucumber sandwiches cut into triangles and I ate one for my tea. Other times I had no tea at all and I went to bed hungry.

She said to me one morning, “These cornflakes belong to me and you are not to touch them,” so I had to go to school without any breakfast again.

I started missing school on purpose because I could not concentrate on my lessons.

I would go to Grandma's house and she would give me jam sandwiches.

One day I refused to go home again and my grandad Mitchell called the police because I looked very thin and my eczema was bad.

The police told my father Geoffrey that I was living at my grandparents' house with them and I would not be returning to live with him and Barbara.

My father Geoffrey came to my grandparents' house and he said to them, "If you have Sandra you will have to take David as well."

So they agreed to have David living with them as well. Thank God my grandparents helped us.

Chapter Twelve: Living With My Grandparents

After this I slowly managed to put the past behind me, as I lived with my grandparents. After a while I hardly thought about the past at all and settled into life with them. I had been through a lot for a child aged nine; all this change and upheaval was not good.

For the future ahead I was going to be happy thanks to grandparents who saved my life when I was on the brink of starving to death.

My address was now 4 Leamington Street, Rochdale. Grandma said that it was her dream house when she had moved in. Grandma and Grandad had lived there for around twenty years.

Her first house when she had first got married had been a terraced house at St John Street. It had no garden either back or front and it was a back to back terraced house. So Grandma dreamed of having her own garden. She watched a television show with a man called Percy Thrower presenting gardening and it was her favourite show.

Grandma had started gardening whilst she lived at 4 Leamington Street and the gardens at the back and the front of the house were superb.

She was sixty years old when we moved in with her and John was sixty-four and he worked as a care assistant at Horse Carrs Nursing Home at Falinge in Rochdale. When he was younger he had worked as an engineer's fitter.

The house had three bedrooms so David had his own room. I shared a bedroom with my grandmother. She did not sleep with her husband John by this time because she said he snored very loudly and it kept her awake all night! So Grandad slept in his own room as well, I used to wonder about when the last time was that they had slept together as a couple. It must have been after my uncle Jack was born in 1933. The Pill had not been invented so Grandma no longer seemed to want sex with Grandad at all after this!

Grandma slept in a double bed on her own and I slept in a single bed in the same room. The beds had flannelette sheets with counterpanes covering the blanket and dark red eiderdowns on top.

Sometimes at night it could be quite cold when I first got into bed because there was no central heating at Grandma's house, and therefore the bedroom was cold.

David and I attended Greenbank Primary School. David was two years below me at school.

I remember going for lunch at Greenbank Primary School. The children all sat on round tables in the dining room. Each table had eight children sat at it; at every table there was placed a brightly coloured jug. Some jugs were bright blue, some were red, others were bright green. I was sitting at a table with a bright blue jug in the middle of the table. I reached for the jug, it contained lovely chilled water, the water had been chilled with ice. I poured some into the glass that sat in front of me. Out poured the cool water and two chunks of ice. I placed the jug back in the middle of the table and instinctively drank the chilled water. It tasted lovely. I liked it there. The other children were really friendly. It felt like I was in a bubble.

Each table queued up for their dinner at the hatch, the dinner ladies were really nice and asked me what I would like for lunch. I recognised one of the dinner ladies as one of my neighbours. It was my friend Wendy Copestick's mum.

Grandma consistently taught us to have manners and be polite at all times.

We were also brought up as Christians.

We would have to say “yes, please” and “no, thank you” at all times.

When we ate our food, we held our knife in our right hand and our fork in our left hand.

The cutlery was set in this way so that the knife was on the right side of the hand and the fork was on the left side. The dessert spoon was placed at the top with the handle facing to the right.

If we were having fish then the table knife would be replaced and replaced with a fish knife.

Soup would be eaten with a round dessert soup spoon!

We would never dribble our food or place our mouths near our plates. The cutlery were the tools to bring the food to our mouths.

We all ate our food at the dining table and meals were always served at certain times of day. The cutlery was always set in the correct way with the knife and fork placed correctly.

We always ate with our mouths closed. If we had to speak for any reason such as asking “Could you please pass the salt?” we had to wait until after we had swallowed our food first before we asked for it. One was never to stretch over at the meal table and always wait and ask for items to be passed. When we had eaten our food and we wanted to leave the table we had to ask, “May I leave the table, please?” then wait to be excused.

In general, we were taught by our grandparents to always show respect to other people and to consider the feelings of others. We had to be polite to others.

We always said “please” and “thank you” when it was appropriate to do so.

We were also taught to respect people especially our elders.

In summer 1968, Grandma said we would be going to stay in Blackpool for a holiday and that we were expected to display our table manners in the hotel where we would be staying.

I was so excited to be going away on a holiday where we would be staying all night in a hotel. I had never done this before, I had only ever been away on day trips.

Of course, I had lived in an orphanage in Derbyshire but I had been living there and not just been on a holiday in Derbyshire.

So going on a proper holiday was completely different from actually living in a place.

Being on holiday would mean that we would be able to do lots of exciting things!

I did not pack straight away because there were still a few days to go before we set off but Grandma liked to be organised.

That night when I went to bed I could not sleep with excitement. I pictured in my mind which clothes I would need to wear on the holiday. We were going for fourteen nights.

I decided that I needed to pack seven dresses so that I could wear a dress for half of the time.

I imagined placing them neatly inside the suitcase. I would be wearing a different one every day. The rest of the time I could wear shorts or slacks and so I took a pair of shorts and three pairs of slacks. One of these had a flowery pattern.

I imagined what all the dresses would look like and where I would be going in them. Grandma said that we would be going to shows in the evenings. Should I have daywear as well as nightwear? I thought.

When I asked Grandma about it she said that I was too young to be dressing up at night. That meant I would wear the same clothes.

Nevertheless, I could still have a different outfit on every day! This took quite a lot of thought for a ten-year-old girl.

David was to share a suit case with Grandad as men and boys did not need as many clothes as girls, Grandma said. Grandma was to have a separate suit case for herself and all her flowery dresses!

After much thought I packed my suitcase carefully. Seven dresses and five pairs of slacks! And then two pairs of shorts for sunny weather!

Finally, we were ready to go to Blackpool for our annual summer holiday, and the first holiday ever for my brother David and myself!

Neither of my grandparents drove a car and we were going to Blackpool on a coach that was called a Yelloway coach. The problem with this was that smoking was allowed on the coaches at the time so the coach smelled of cigarette smoke and I used to feel sick on the coach and I said to Grandma, "Can we get off this coach and walk to Blackpool?"

Of course, this was not possible because Blackpool was too far to walk to. It was fifty miles from where we lived in Rochdale.

Grandma always said that the summer weather in England lasted until the middle of

September. She said she knew this because her birthday was on the thirteenth of September and every year of her life it had been sunny on her birthday!

Therefore, she said she always went on her annual summer holidays within the first two weeks in September.

My grandparents had been going to Blackpool for their holidays for several years.

Grandma always liked to visit Stanley Park in Blackpool where she would gain ideas on how to design her own garden at Leamington Street.

We always booked into the same boarding house which was called Craigards and it was in the central part of Blackpool, quite near to the Blackpool Tower.

Neither of my grandparents had ever been abroad. They had both travelled to other seaside resorts in England when they had been children but since they were married they always went to Blackpool together. They said there was so much to see and do in Blackpool. Grandma said, "Even if it rains you can go in the penny arcade in the Winter Gardens."

When we were in Blackpool in 1970 we went to see Ken Dodd and his Diddy Men. The Diddy Men skipped onto the stage singing:

We are the diddy men, Doddy's little diddy men, we are the diddy men and we come from Knotty Ash!

Then Dodd would tell a few jokes and we were in stitches laughing along with the audience.

The next night we went to the pictures to see a new screen version of *Oliver!*, which was a musical starring Mark Lester as Oliver and Jack Wild as the Artful Dodger. This is still one of my favourite films.

After this holiday every year in early September, David and I went on holiday to Blackpool with our grandparents until we grew up.

I felt quite grown up in my purple dress with tights on and red leather shoes and a new black leather handbag.

Chapter Thirteen: Greenbank Primary School

David and I attended Greenbank Primary School which is on Greenbank Road in Rochdale.

David was in a different year group to myself. I did not really see much of him during the day apart from the morning assembly when the whole school gathered in the hall to sing hymns such as, *All things bright and beautiful* and we said prayers such as the Lord's Prayer, 'Our Father who art in heaven.'

Sometimes I saw him at playtime. He had his own group of friends and was settling into school well.

I was making a few friends as well but this was hard because the other children already knew each other by the time that I arrived to be with them in their year group.

Nevertheless, I was quite outgoing and sociable and Anne had said I was always resilient as a child.

My teacher here was called Miss Russell and she often smelled of Germolene.

I didn't know why she smelled of Germolene and I never asked her why as I was taught to be very polite. I just used to think, "Miss Russell smells of Germolene again."

Maybe she had a heat rash and sometimes she looked slightly flushed as well.

She was a kind lady who took us for sewing and embroidery. Miss Russell said that I had good sewing fingers because my fingers are long.

When I went to this school I learned sewing, embroidery and dressmaking in Miss Russell's class.

I made a yellow blouse and matching wrap-over skirt whilst attending this class.

Miss Russell showed me how to use a paper pattern to complete the design that I would be sewing. The paper pattern was a paper blouse and a paper wrap-over skirt for a ten-year-old girl. I chose yellow cotton for the material. The idea was to cut the material as per the exact size of the paper pattern because the pattern was exactly my size and for a ten-year-old girl. (picture)

When it was finished it looked really good. I felt proud that I had made it myself.

I took the yellow blouse and matching wrap-over skirt in my suit case to Blackpool with me to wear as one of my daily outfits!

Miss Russell also showed me how to do embroidery using a silk thread on an embroidery mat. These mats could be used to make coasters for resting hot drinks on.

Miss Russell was about medium height and rather plump. Her hair was in shampoo and set mode and it reminded me of my grandma's hair.

Her hair was platinum blonde. She would have been about sixty years old.

Sometimes in those days women that wanted a career had to choose between a domestic home life and a career, and if they chose a career they had to not get married. Miss Russell reminded me of women in this category.

On Saturdays I attended 'BBC minors' at the Rochdale pictures in Rochdale town centre. This later became Wetherspoons.

I remember David and I queueing outside the pictures for it to open. All the kids were getting excited outside the pictures and a lot of them had started screaming and shouting waiting for the pictures to open and some of them had started playing tig.

This is where you tig someone and then run off so they have to chase you and catch you in order to tig you back.

Eventually we would be allowed in as the hour approached 10 o'clock and the queue started to go down as the children went into the pictures and paid their shilling at the kiosk and went up the stairs to find a seat.

The film showing could be *Chitty Chitty Bang Bang* or *Mary Poppins.*

The kids that went were all around the same age. We all thought that it was great and everyone was really excited because we didn't know which film we would be watching. Once it was *Whistle Down the Wind* about some children finding a hungry man in a barn, not realising that he was an escaped convict and all the children want to look after him because they think he is Jesus.

We used to sing a song called *ABC minors.* We sang the song when we were all seated in our seats and before the film came on. This way we all felt that we all belonged in the club.

Sometimes there was a showing of Laurel and Hardy the comedians and they were among David's favourites. He used to laugh in hysterics all the way through it.

David loved comedy shows and loved to watch *Steptoe and Son*. I didn't know it then but I realised later that David watched comedy shows as he found them therapeutic.

On Sundays David and I attended Hope Street Chapel and Sunday school.

Grandma did not take us there, we went there on our own. It was only at the back of where we lived at Leamington Street. It was called a chapel but it was exactly like a church inside. There were benches made out of dark oak wood. The vicar said a sermon and the congregation sang hymns.

The children stayed after the sermon and hymn singing for Sunday school, which was mainly colouring in colouring books about stories of the miracles that Jesus performed.

The church and Sunday school went on until about three o'clock and then David and I went home to our grandparents' house. It was only a five minute walk back.

Grandma always cooked a Sunday roast dinner for us whilst we had been away at church. This was usually a roast chicken which would have been purchased the day before. In those days there were no home freezers. Grandma had a fridge for fresh food. I was fascinated with the pantry. I thought it was too small to keep food in. This is where a lot of tinned foods were stored. It was built into the living room and looked like a small cupboard by the window.

Sometimes she made her own custard pie. It was a particular favourite of Grandad's!

It was made using fresh eggs.

Grandma had many talents which seem to be less popular now. She had skills such as knitting and dressmaking. This meant that she made most of her own clothes including her dresses and she knitted jumpers, especially when she was younger.

By the time David and I went to live with her she was not as active as she had been when she was younger, she lost some of her stamina with age, but she still did gardening and a bit of sewing on a Singer sewing machine.

One day she even made cushion covers out of some old living room curtains. I came home from school and said, "Grandma, didn't these cushion covers used to be the curtains?"

She replied, "Yes, the curtains were tatty and I was going to throw them away but decided to make them into cushion covers instead."

She had sewn them on her Singer sewing machine.

The curtains as cushion covers looked very effective, they were a flamboyant pattern of pink flowers with a cream-coloured background. Grandma hardly ever threw anything away and she was always "making do."

At the window she had replaced the old curtains with a pale pink flowery pair that were slightly less worn!

At school I met some children who I was to know for the rest of my life. One of the girls I met was called Robina Walker. She was one of my friends. I went to her house one Saturday, she lived at St Anne's Road in Rochdale, along with her parents Ruby and Samuel Walker. She had four siblings named John, Marion, Fiona and Belinda.

When I went to her house her mother served me a piece of toast which she spread with Stork margarine. I never tasted Stork margarine before, or any other kind of margarine because my grandma always used Lurpak butter.

I liked the taste of the Stork margarine as it had a unique taste.

Some of the children I met I lost contact with and others I heard about for years afterwards through the grapevine.

At Greenbank School I remember the girls' toilets and the sinks all in a row! There was buttermilk soap on the sinks. This must have been left on the sinks by the council, whose cleaners were the caretakers for the toilets and washroom. When I washed my hands with the soap it was a comforting smell and the smell of buttermilk soap always reminds me of Greenbank Primary School and my time there.

At Christmas 1967 I was invited to the annual Christmas party at Greenbank Primary School.

"Grandma," I said, "I have been invited to the Christmas party at school and I want to go."

Grandma said I could not go because it meant walking through the streets at night to get to the school.

Then Grandad said, "I'll go next door and ask Jack if he will take Sandra to the party."

And off he went next door to ask my uncle. I was excited about going because I was a young child that loved to socialise and I had not been at the school long so it was a chance to make stronger friendships.

My uncle Jack said he would take me to the Christmas party as it was after he had finished work for the day. He worked as a foreman at Whipp and Bourne engineering in Rochdale. By this time, he and his wife Yvonne had three children and they had moved in next door at 2 Leamington Street, which was a garden-fronted end terrace.

I went to the annual Christmas party and afterwards my uncle collected me from my grandma's where I had now taken up permanent residence and was a very happy child at this time of my childhood.

Miss Russell told all the children to bring a bag of sugar to the school the week before the Christmas holidays in 1968. She said it did not matter whether it was a one pound or a two pound bag of sugar.

She showed us how to wrap it up carefully in tin foil which was a great idea because the clingfilm clung to the bag of sugar and made it look like a perfect rectangle shape and the chunkiness of the present made it look like an exciting Christmas gift.

Miss Russell said we should give the bag of sugar to someone that we knew, so I gave mine to the two Mrs Wards. They said it was the loveliest Christmas gift that they had ever had.

In 1967 at Christmas time, we were also invited to the nursing home where my grandad worked for their annual Christmas party. We attended this as a family of four, that is my grandma, grandad, brother David and myself. We went to Horse Carrs where Grandad worked as a care assistant. It was on Falinge Road in Rochdale.

Grandad said to some of the old people, "These are my grandchildren, Sandra and David, who have come to live with us."

Then Grandma said, "Their mother has died so they live with us."

This is when Grandma would begin to make me feel very embarrassed and I wished that she wouldn't put us on display in this way.

The older people enjoyed meeting David and I, as Grandad said that they didn't have many visitors.

The older people were always made a fuss of at Christmas and Father Christmas arrived to give them all token presents and David received a board game with Ludo on one side of the cardboard and snakes and ladders on the other side. Both games were played using a dice and tiddlywinks.

I was given a little dressing up doll made of paper, first you had to cut out the doll and then cut the dress out and fasten it to the doll with little tabs. I really liked this because I was beginning to have a keen interest in fashion.

One of the boys was called Stuart Milne, who was a popular young man when he grew up.

Another of the boys I met back then was called Kirk Gartside. He used to help me with my drawings at school. I had an interest in drawing at the time. Kirk used to tell me which drawings he thought I had done best. These were drawings of fashionable clothes.

Then there was Colin Yates. I saw him years later on Rochdale inside market. He had his own hardware store and sold metal pans and suchlike.

Grandma was always very proud of her garden.

In the back garden she had a lawn of rich green grass where we would play and it was surrounded by flower beds containing sweet peas, tulips, daffodils and roses, all of which had the most invigorating scent.

Grandma's favourite flowers were roses and she grew these in bushes and in a variety of colours. They were often giant roses that smelled of the most alluring scent.

She was often to be found amongst the flower beds attending to her beautiful flowers.

Every morning after she retired, Grandma would be out in the garden very early attending to the beautiful flowers and flower beds. She had the gift of green fingers and every year the flowers bloomed.

In the spring following the winter frost the flowers would come out following the early appearance of daffodils which always represent the coming of spring.

I went out into the garden and asked Grandma what she was doing and she said she was mainly getting rid of the weeds from amongst the flower beds.

Grandma said that flowers were like human beings They came from buds and then they bloomed for a short time and then they died.

I said, "No, Grandma, this is not true. When I am at church I have learned that humans can live for ever."

How could Grandma send me to church and then say she didn't even believe in God herself?

Had David been right when he said she just sent us to church and Sunday school so that we would be out of the way on Sundays? I did not want to believe this as I always thought the very best about Grandma. In my eyes she had saved us from peril.

We lived at 4 Leamington Street and went to school and then went home again and life was relatively normal again, just like it had been when my mother was alive and we had lived just over the road.

Every morning before I left to go to school I would kiss my grandma goodbye because I needed to let her know how much I needed her.

Grandma said that David and I were allowed to start having a comic delivered once a week. I chose *Bunty* and David had *The Beano*. His favourite story was 'Pansy Potter, the Strong Man's Daughter.' She was very strong. He also read 'Dennis the Menace' in his comic. It was about a boy that was always up to mischief and was very naughty most of the time! David, in contrast, was a quiet person but he was a good pupil at school and was very good at mathematics. Grandma called him a 'good scholar' which is an old-fashioned term for someone who is good at studying at school.

My favourite story in my *Bunty* comic was about a girl called Flipper Feet who had big feet so this made her a good swimmer. Every week I read my comic to see what happened to her next. She entered swimming races and liked to win them. I also liked the cut out dolls and cut out clothes.

Chapter Fourteen: Redbrook School, 1969

In September 1969 I started at a new school called Redbrook Middle School in Rochdale. I was eleven years old and due to be twelve in November.

Grandma was sent a letter through the post that I had to be dressed in a school uniform at the start of term. The letter that came explained what the uniform was and advised my guardian, who was Grandma, where we would be more likely to be able to buy the uniform from.

I was very excited and looked forward to picking and wearing a school uniform because I had never worn one before!

The list said I should have:

- A long-sleeved pale blue blouse
- A navy-blue pleated skirt
- A navy-blue cardigan
- A red tie

This was the list for day wear.

Then there was a list that I should have for games and P.E:

- A short-sleeved Airtex blouse
- A wrap-over navy skirt
- White socks
- A pair of pumps

So one day during the long summer holidays we set off to a shop called Trumans, which was on Drake Street in Rochdale.

We went inside the shop and were greeted by the assistant.

Grandma handed her the list of things that I needed to start at Redbrook School.

The assistant said that she would have to take a few measurements from me. She took out a tape measure from her pocket and measured my waist and the length from my waist to my knee for the skirt measurement.

At Redbrook Middle School, I met a girl named Julie Withington who became my best friend.

I met Julie on the first day at the school in the dining hall at dinner time.

The year group that I was in were allocated dining tables at dinner time.

Julie came up to the table holding her finger which she had cut. She said, “Does anyone know where the first aid office is?”

Another pupil said, “Have you cut your finger?” and the girl that was holding her right forefinger with her left hand said, “Yes, I cut it on a pencil sharpener.”

Then the other girl said the first aid office was where the nurse was, next to the main office.

Julie said that she did not know where the main office was. I knew where the first aid office was and that it was next door to the main school office. When I was touring the school prior to my attendance there I remembered this information from the person who had showed me round the school. I remembered because I thought I might need to go to first aid myself if my eczema flared up.

So I took Julie to the first aid office for a plaster. Julie looked like she needed someone to help her as she was also feeling strange in a new environment and so was I but I had been through quite a lot of upheaval in my life by this time and I was taking this new day at yet another new school in my stride!

So Julie became my best friend at Redbrook Middle School, which was on Bridefold Road in Rochdale.

We had drama lessons in ‘the hall’ and we had a scene where one of us was a stone statue and the other one was a witch doctor bringing the statue to life. First Julie was the statue and I played the part of the witch doctor. The theme tune to this drama was from *The Good, the Bad and the Ugly.*

I had to dance around the statue, bringing it back to life bit by bit until it was dancing in unison with me.

So the witch doctor brought the statue back to life after a few minutes; he had breathed fresh life into the statue and it had now returned to being a human being.

Then it was Julie's turn to be the witch doctor and I became the statue. I was crouched down and still when the music started to play again. After one verse of the music ended the chorus began to play and this was my cue to begin unwinding and become more and more aware of my surroundings as I came to life.

I met several other girls whilst I was at Redbrook Middle School and I sometimes felt that they seemed to be older than me.

We were all eleven but a lot of them were bigger in body and more mature than me for their age.

We were all growing into adolescents and were all in our twelfth year. A few of the girls would talk about boys that they had met and perhaps were dating.

At school I excelled in music, religious studies and English and every year I came first or second in all of these subjects.

All the school had been split into four groups. These were St Andrews (Scotland) who were the blue team. St Patricks (Ireland) were the green team. St George (England) wore the colour red. Finally, there was the Welsh team of St David, who wore the colour yellow for competing at games.

I was in St David's team but I did not enter any major sporting competitions. Once a week Mr Langley's class went to the public baths at Rochdale to start swimming lessons. A coach came for the children and our class went after lunch.

I went as well although I could swim already through being taught at the orphanage. I never told anyone that I used to live in an orphanage because I wanted to fit in with my peers.

I enjoyed the swimming lessons and gained a certificate for swimming the length of the pool.

Sometimes the swimming was a sporting event with the four houses of the school competing against each other so Julie and I spectated instead along with the rest of our class.

I settled into the school but I was aware that a lot of the girls in the same year as me seemed older and bigger in height than me. They mostly saw me as a swot as I was very good in English class. I also excelled at religious studies and every year I came first or second in the class. A couple of the other girls in the class were annoyed about this. These few girls thought that because they were loud that they should be top of the class at everything. I was one of the quieter people so they thought that I should be behind academically as well, but this was not the case.

With the help of the music teacher Miss Purdy, I learned to play the recorder so well that within a few months I was a contestant at the Rochdale music festival at Rochdale College.

On the actual day of the music festival, I did not attend school because Grandma took me to the Rochdale College music festival instead.

The children that attended the concert were sat with their parents.

The first child was eventually called to the stage to perform their piece of music on the recorder.

Then it was the turn of the second piece and it was a duet with two girls playing their well-rehearsed ensemble.

After they had completed it the audience applauded with much delight as the girls quietly made their way off the stage.

Eventually it was my turn to play my piece of music on my recorder.

I heard my name being called from the front of the audience, which was made up mostly of the mums and dads of the children playing a musical instrumental piece.

I closed the pamphlet and calmly passed it to my grandma, who looked at me nervously. I smiled a smile at her that said, "Don't worry" and walked towards the stage holding my recorder, which I had polished well the evening before.

I went up the steps to the stage and stood still when I arrived at the book stand. I did not have a music book with me as I was only playing one short piece and I had rehearsed it very well.

I had my recorder ready and it looked like a long stick pointing at the audience.

Instinctively I knew not to look at anyone and especially not to have any eye contact with any of the members of the audience as this would throw me off balance and I would have lost concentration.

Instead, I focused on the very end section of my recorder and placed my fingers on the notes.

As I played I focussed on the same focal point. It was above someone's head.

I started the verse, 'Speed bonny boat' and the music rang out around the hall.

Concentrating on the focal point I carried on playing the piece of music:

Speed bonny boat
Like a bird on the wing
Onward the sailors cry
Carry the lad that's born to be king
Over the sea to Skye

Loud the winds howl
Loud the waves roar
Thunderclaps fill the air
Baffled our foes
Stand by the shores
Follow they will not dare

The Skye Boat Song is a Scottish Jacobite song about Bonnie Prince Charlie.

I managed to complete the piece of music on my recorder.

I took a modest little bow and left the stage to an applauding audience.

For my performance I achieved a 'first class certificate of merit' for my solo piece.

After this I kept up my music lessons and learned to read music.

I could play the recorder and I wanted to learn the flute one day.

My lovely friend Julie invited me to her house one day. She had long blonde hair and a face that reminded me of a chicken. This is because she had big blue eyes, a pointed nose and a receding chin. She was a very kind and loyal friend.

I went to her house one dinnertime from school.

She lived in a large semi-detached house surrounded by a well-kept garden.

Julie was the eldest of three children and lived with her parents. Her father ran a carpet shop in Rochdale. It was on Yorkshire Street in Rochdale and it was called Empress Hall Carpets.

When I went into Julie's I thought the rooms were bigger and brighter than the house where I lived. Even so, I was happy living with my grandparents.

Her family had two toilets and one of them was downstairs.

Julie said to me, "Look at what I have to wear," and she showed me some sanitary products that were in the downstairs toilet.

I asked, “What do you have those for, Julie?” and she explained to me that she had started her periods.

I did not know what she meant as Grandma had never explained to me about girls having periods. I was grateful to Julie for explaining this to me as I was being brought up in a rather old-fashioned way!

Grandma did not want to talk to me about periods or boys or even about growing up at all. It was as if she always wanted me to remain a child, but this was not realistic.

When I did games at Redbrook School my class all went in the changing room to get changed into our games kit.

Most of the girls were wearing a small adolescent bra, usually size 32 in an A cup, but I was wearing a vest!

I tried to get changed as quickly as possible so that no one noticed that I was wearing a child’s vest even though I was now becoming an adolescent!

The girls played hockey and they were very sporty. Once a week we all did cross country running and I was good at this because I was small and skinny. We would all set off running across the school field and down a dirt track at the side of the school and then onto Bury Road which is a busy main road. We ran on this for about a mile before turning onto Sandy Lane and kept running and running until we came to Bridgefold Road which is where our school was. By the time we got to this point I had left most of the other girls behind, so when I reached the school I quickly made my way to the girls' changing rooms and hurriedly got dressed before anyone noticed that I had a vest on!

I told Grandma that I wanted a bra so that I could look like the other girls. She said, "You don't have a bust at all and you are too young to wear a bra."

"Well, Grandma, I could wear a crop top."

But she still said no.

At the time I was twelve years old. I was small and skinny and did not look my age.

I led a much more sheltered life than any of my peers at school and the generation gap between my grandparents and myself was apparent. Still, I loved and respected them both and I do not know what David and I would ever have done without them and I was always grateful to them. David said he wished we lived with our mum and dad like everyone else at school. Sometimes their old-fashioned ideas got on David's nerves but we had to accept this and we were both very polite and well-mannered. It even crossed my mind that I was too polite!

Our games teacher at Redrook School was called Miss Sharrocks. She was a well-built and very energetic lady with blonde hair. She was someone that you did not mess with. She dressed in a white mini skirt over very muscly calves.

Sometimes during games at school, I had to be excluded if the weather became too hot for me. My skin would start to itch and feel dry. I had to go to First Aid and the nurse put Nulon moisturiser on my arms and legs. I could not do games like hockey so I used to watch the other girls play instead. I sat under a tree in the shade! Miss Sharrocks would teach the girls to give the ball such a good batting with their rounders bats!

When I batted the ball I often missed because the rounders bat was more like a truncheon than a bat and I still had to run to the post whether I managed to hit the ball or not.

Our house of St David did very well at games and came first in the school most years. We would be awarded a trophy that was displayed in the sports hall and all the girls got a badge for their parents to stitch onto their games kit. Our house had yellow badges.

I had French lessons at Redbrook Middle School and our teacher was Mr Burn.

I enjoyed these lessons and I could speak a little French after having lessons for about a year. I learned the names of shops such as *la boucherie,* which is a butcher's shop?

And I learned "*Quel age avez vous?*" which is asking your age in French.

The lessons were designed to help us to get by in French if we ever went on holiday to France. At the time I had never been abroad but they were to help me later.

One day in our French lesson Mr Burn said that we had all been allocated a pen friend in France. Julie and I were really excited about this.

Mr Burn said we should write a letter saying our age and where we lived and what our hobbies were and we would send the letter to a similar person in France along with our photograph. Also, our letters had to be written in French.

This was our project for the week. Julie and I met up on the Saturday so that we could have our photo taken at a photo booth. We had separate photos taken to send to our new pen friend in France, our photos were both black and white and just of our head and shoulders. I was very excited about writing a letter in French to a girl my age that lived in France.

Mr Burn told everyone what their pen friend's name was and my pen friend was called Therese.

Cher Therese,
Comment allez vous?
Je m'appelle Sandra, j'ai douze ans.
J'aimerais aller en France.
Quelle est votre matière preferee a l'ecole?
A l'ecole j'aime mieux la musique parce que
J'aime jouer mon enregistreur.
Je voudrais visiter une patisserie.

This translates to;

'Dear Therese
How are you?
My name is Sandra and I am twelve years old.
I would love to go to France.
What is your favourite subject at school?
My favourite subject at school is music because I like playing my recorder.
I would love to visit a cake shop in France.'

Therese and I exchanged one or two letters but I did not meet her or go to France.

But I always kept her passport photograph that she sent to me.

Chapter Fifteen: 1970

In late September of 1970, Miss Purdy, our music teacher, said she wanted to group together a choir to start rehearsals for singing at the parish church in Rochdale town centre.

The choir would be singing at Christmas and she only wanted people to join the choir who would be committed to practising and able to be present at the parish church for three evenings during the Christmas period.

Some people said they could not do it but those that could stayed behind to start practising. I decided to stay behind and I joined the choir. My friend Julie did join at first and later she decided that she didn't want to do it and so she dropped out.

However, I carried on and we practised singing at the parish church one dinnertime every week.

The singing practice involved meeting up during lunchtime once a week

So we did appear at the parish church.

I was stood on the second row of singing schoolchildren because I was amongst the smallest but the children on the front row were smaller than me.

We sang Christmas carols.

The first two rows of singers, which included myself, sang the harmonies.

During our last year at Redbrook School my best friend Julie and I were chosen, along with a few other pairs of girls from the year, to take assembly in the mornings.

The school held a Christian assembly every week day at school and it was held first thing in the morning.

Julie and I took turns at making announcements about the school, introducing the next hymn to be sung and prayers to be offered.

In our last year at Redbrook Middle School when we were having one of our last lessons in religious studies with our teacher Mr Charnley, he announced that I had come either first or second in both English and religious studies for the last two years at the school.

One girl in the class named Elaine Rhodes started grumbling about this and said, "Why has Sandra come first or second in English and religious studies for two years when she doesn't know anything at all about sex?"

I smiled at them both and I thought, "I'm too polite, Grandma!"

www.ingramcontent.com/pod-product-compliance
Ingram Content Group UK Ltd.
Pitfield, Milton Keynes, MK11 3LW, UK
UKHW020414250726
13967UKWH00007B/2645

9 781800 310537